Dedication

This book of devotions is dedicated to my Lord and Savior Who is not content to leave me as I am, and Who deserves all my devotion.

Keep Going

I often find myself at the side of a hospital bed or observing a speech therapy session or watching a grueling hour of physical therapy with my children.

Nearly every time, my mouth opens to say "Keep going! You can do it! You have come so far already! Don't stop! I know it is so hard, but it will all be worth it soon! I am right here with you!"

Today, when I have been so discouraged with my inability to be all the things my "people" need me to be, overwhelmed with all that must be done, and I have felt so "less than", the Holy Spirit whispered to me, "Keep going! You can do it! You have come so far already! Don't stop! I know it is so hard, but it will all be worth it soon! I am right here with you!"

If you are reading this, and you are one of His children, He is saying that to you today. He is with us. We can keep going with His help.

It will all be worth it soon.

Further Reading

Hebrews 12, James 1

Journal Space

Pity Party

I have been having a big, old pity party lately. Ever been there…when you just cannot get your mind off a bad thing? You know Jesus could fix it, but He is not doing it.

Well, I have been there for the last little while. Today, the Holy Spirit finally said, "Hey, Mindy, do you know what a luxury it is to get to have a pity party?"

Huh?! But I started thinking about that. Do you think people searching for resources have time for a pity party? If I have time for a pity party, it means my needs have been met, and I have time on my hands to think about my wants. It means I have experienced the joy of someone or something if I am pouting about losing them/it. It means I have chosen to dwell on what I am missing instead on what I have been given. What a spoiled brat!

So as my sweet friend Fran likes to say, "Today I will live in the promise…not in the lack."

The Lord promises to see me, know me, and meet my needs…even though I am never deserving. I'm done with the pity party. I will live in His promise, because He is good!

Further Reading

Philippians 4:10-23, I Peter 1:3

Journal Space

A Matter of Trust

When I talk to my six year old daughter Amyra, and she wants to emphasize that what she is telling me is true, she will say "I am trusting you!"

I asked her why she says, "I am trusting you" instead of saying "I am telling the truth." Her response..."I am trusting you to know what the truth is!"

Goodness, how I need to hear that! When I pray and talk to the Lord, am I trusting Him to know what the truth is? Am I trying to convince Him that I know truth better?

My heart is so easily fooled...often by the good things that are simply not the best things.

God knows the truth of my sinfulness. He knows the truth of my future...failures and successes. He knows the truth of my needs and my wants (so often confused in my heart).

God knows the truth, and I am trusting Him!

Further Reading

Proverbs 3:5-8, Psalm 37:5, Matthew 7:11, Isaiah 26:3

Journal Space

Family

Amyra just called to me from the next room. When I got there, she was sitting next to her brother, Hudson and she said, "Hudson needs his nose wiped."

I looked at her and said "You are right next to him. Wipe his nose!"

"That's not really my job."

"Amyra, we are a FAMILY. When we see that one of us needs help, we help them. It doesn't matter if that is our regular job or not!' I was completely astounded that she had expected me to come help her brother when she was next to him and capable of helping him herself!

Then, as it often happens, the Holy Spirit began to speak to my heart.

Am I expecting someone else to help my brother or sister when I am next to them and perfectly capable of helping?

Am I writing a note of encouragement or expecting someone else to do it?

Am I praying or expecting someone else to pray?

Am I giving aid or expecting it to come from someone else?

And the list goes on and on. I have been on the end of needing help (at times receiving it, at times not receiving it), and I know the smallest things make such a difference.

It may not be our "regular" job, but we need to help those in need when God brings our paths together. We need to look at the brother or sister next to us to take note of his or her need.

After all, we are a family.

Further Reading

John 13:34-35, Romans 13:8-10, Luke 10:25-37

Journal Space

Vision of Jesus

You might know that our son Hudson has Fetal Alcohol Syndrome (among other challenges). You might know that Hudson is Caucasian, blonde, and blue-eyed. You might NOT know that doctors, nurses, and health care providers are often not aware upon first meeting us that we are not biological mother and son.

Until they are informed that he is adopted, they often (99% of the time) treat me as the lowest of the low…disdain just dripping off them.

Every single time this happens, I think "Yeah, that's how Jesus would treat a woman in this position."

Then I think "Yeah, you never judge anyone without knowing all the facts. You never think you are better than someone, just because you don't happen to have the same issue. You never hold yourself up as the epitome of morality compared to others' sinfulness."

Listen, I DO NOT condone sin. As a matter of fact, I would probably have a few choice words to say to Hudson's biological mother about what she has done to him…but when are we going to start looking at people and saying, "Jesus loves them, so I will, too"?

So, every time this happens to me, I am that more determined not to be the one doing it to someone else.

My prayer is that we followers of Jesus will ask Him to help us love others the way He does…and that we would stop dissecting sin and start disseminating love.

Further Reading

I Corinthians 13, Mark 12:33, I John 4:7-9

Journal Space

His Plans

"For I know the plans that I have for you,' declares the LORD, 'plans for welfare and not for calamity to give you a future and a hope'." Jeremiah 29:11

We have all read that Scripture a million times. But have you read it this way...HE knows the plans HE has for you?

I am a planner by nature. My family jokes that when I say that I have been thinking, they should just go get in the car...because I have a plan, and we are all going to go out and get it done!

If I had planned my life, I would have been married at age 21 to a Free Will Baptist man that was around my age. I would have then proceeded to have 3 children who were little angels that had only "normal" problems. I would always be well-liked and well-thought-of by everyone. No issues in our lives...easy.

Instead, HE planned to have me get married at age 27 to a former Methodist that was 8 years older than I am. I did not get to have the 3 "normal" biological children. Instead, HE planned for me to **work** crazy hard at adopting and mothering **2** special needs sweethearts. I never **planned** to spend my days driving from orthotics fittings to speech therapy sessions to physical therapy sessions to cardiology and pulmonology and endocrinology and nutritionist appointments...and then get up and do it all over again the next day...while working in time for vision exercises, PT and speech exercises, feeding by mouth exercises, etc. But that was always part of what HE planned.

Why?

Well have you ever read the verses that come after Jeremiah 29:11?

"THEN you will call upon Me and come and pray to Me, and I will listen to you. You will seek Me and find Me when you search for Me with all your heart. I will be found by you,' declares the LORD'." Jeremiah 29:12-14a

Because if it all went how I planned, I would never look to HIM! He knew that if my plans were always successful, I would have felt that I had no need to turn to my Savior. I would have no need to grow or be stretched or realize that I cannot do everything myself. I need Him. And HE (not the life I had planned) is my great reward!

I would have missed out on this beautiful family, the miracles that came with them, and an intimate knowledge of Who it is I am really serving and what He (not I) is capable of doing.

I cried out to Him. He heard me. I found Him. All because HE had plans for me so much better than my own.

So, don't be discouraged when your life seems to be a mess. That's when you can be sure…HE has plans for you!

Further Reading

Jeremiah 29:11-14a, Romans 8:28, Deuteronomy 4:29-31a

Be Glad

There are times when you believe that you have gotten over something only to have the hurt, pain, disappointment, betrayal, bitterness, etc. rise up in you again suddenly.

When that happens, BE GLAD! If it were up to us, we would go along pretending things were fine forever. But when these feeling spring up anew, we can turn them over to God…admit that we don't know how to get over it…and let Him do a miracle in our hearts.

I am not glad that I am going through this today, but I am so THANKFUL that God loves me too much to pretend that I am all right. He wants more for me than living this way! And no matter what others may do, He loves me and calls me worthy!

"He heals the broken hearted and binds up their wounds. Great is our Lord and abundant in strength; His understanding is infinite." Psalm 147:3

Further Reading

Jeremiah 49:17a, John 14:26, Psalm 147

Amazon

Do you ever order from Amazon? I love the little tracker they provide. I can click on it any time to see where my stuff is and how close it is getting to being delivered.

Ever wish God had an Amazon tracker? Do you (like me) want to know where He is in the process of delivering on His promises? Do you wish you could check to see why He wasn't bringing certain things to your doorstep exactly when you want?

Living by faith and in faith just doesn't work that way. I Corinthians 13:12 says "For now we see in a mirror dimly, but then face to face; now I know in part, but then I will know fully just as I also have been fully known."

It is hard to wait, but I am so thankful I serve a powerful God…with a 100% delivery record. He has never failed to come through.

Amazon just doesn't hold up against that.

Further Reading

2 Corinthians 1:20, Joshua 21:45, Psalm 130

Journal Space

This Year

This year has not been my favorite. Lots of hard things have been put on our family, and the strain has been severe at times.

But I have learned a few things that have helped me.

1. Do what you are doing for Jesus. People will be mean and ungrateful and demanding. Situations will seem impossible. "Undeserved" heartbreak and troubles will come – more than imaginable. But if you are serving Jesus, you do not walk alone, and the things of this world will "fade in the light of His glory and grace." Serving Him is always worth it!
2. Remember how hard it was and how people were to you. If going through difficult things has any purpose, let it be a message to each of us. Let it teach us how to be grateful and kind when we are the ones in need. Let it remind us that if it were not for God's grace and mercy, we could be so far removed from where we are now. Remember how hurtful people were – not to dwell on the hurt, but to determine in your own heart never to be that way to others.
3. All of the hard times are just passing time. This is not our home. We have a home in heaven. So, don't waste time worrying about the things here that are hard or out of control. Serve Him with a happy heart, knowing you are just biding time till you see Him face to face.
4. Celebrate the people and blessings God has given you in the midst of struggle. It is NEVER all bad. God has placed people in your life that help and encourage you. Do not forget to thank them and show them your love. And count your blessings daily (sometimes hourly)! Remind yourself that His blessings ALWAYS outweigh the hard things in our lives.

I don't have it all figured out, but I am learning to rely on the One who does and trust Him completely.

Further Reading

Psalm 9, Psalm 16, I Peter 5:7

Abundance

Every new year, I think about what went well in the past year and what I might want to do differently in the coming year.

Abundant life has been on my mind. I feel like sometimes, we (I) think, "I will finally be living that abundant life when _____ happens." The debt is paid off…the weight is lost…the new house is attained…the illness is cured…the Bible reading/prayer regime is achieved…or _____.

This year, I am convicted that living the abundant life starts NOW…in the midst of struggle. I am not waiting for something to change or improve. He has already given me that abundant life in Him. Yes, I need to be a good steward of what He has given me (body, mind, time, resources, etc.), but that includes living life abundantly with Him…using my struggling life as an example of what He can do – to bring Him honor and glory.

So, it's not going to be abundant when _____. It's abundant now!

Further Reading

Romans 5:17, 2 Corinthians 9:8, Psalm 36:8

Journal Space

Faith Like a Child

(sayings of Carolea Amyra)

"Why do we close our eyes when we pray? What if Jesus does something, and we miss it cause our eyes are closed?"

"I can't spend all my money. What if God or someone else needs some of it?"

"Mom, who thought up 'translucence'? Like jellyfish and the wings on my toy pony. Was it God? He comes up with some AWESOME stuff!"

Upon hearing that not everyone knew that Jesus loved them…"Then we've got to go tell them!"

"Mom, why do people talk about all the ways everyone is different? God made ALL of us people. I don't think the other stuff is very important."

"Mom, how do I stop being angry?"

"Forgive."

"Got any other ideas?"

I corrected Amyra and she said, "God told me the same thing yesterday. Have you guys been talking about me behind my back?"

When we have faith like a child, it is honest. It asks questions. It causes us to want to learn. It causes us to see Him at work in our everyday lives.

I don't want to "be like Mike". I want to be like Amyra, because she is trying to learn how to be like Jesus, and she isn't ashamed of not knowing it all already.

Further Reading

Hebrews 11, Mark 10:14-16

What I Want Is...

The week Amyra was turning 6, nearly every conversation began with "For my birthday, I want..." So, I finally said, "You always get lots of nice things for your birthday, and you already have so many nice things. I want you to stop telling me what you want for your birthday."

A few minutes later, she said, "For my birthday, I mean for my 7TH birthday, I want..."

How often that is me spiritually...never able to focus on all the good things God has already done. Instead, I am all too often looking at the next thing He can do for me.

Lord, thank You for all the many ways You have blessed me...the blessings I wanted and the blessings I needed. Oh, how good You are to give us what we need instead of always what we want! Let me dwell on You and all You have done, that I might be surprised by the next blessing I never saw coming. And may I seek out ways to give for You.

Further Reading

Galatians 4:15, Ephesians 1:3, Matthew 5

Journal Space

Witness

I have always found it very difficult to find natural ways to share my faith with strangers. I am not outgoing, and I do not want to offend others. I avoid conflict whenever possible. I have long struggled with this way of living out my faith.

But now we are adoptive parents.

We are often asked about our children and their medical "situations" and their adoptions. Inevitably, this leads to one of us saying, "God has done so many miracles in our lives!"

And it suddenly occurs to me that God never called me to preach to strangers. He has called us to share what He has done and is doing in our lives.

No fear. No pressure. Just saying, "See this? God did it."

Don't worry that you can't find a certain Bible verse. Don't worry about forgetting one of the Ten Commandments. Tell them what He has done! He has done much! And we are blessed every time He gives us the opportunity to tell how good He is.

Further Reading

Luke 21:13-15, Luke 24:46-48

Journal Space

Scars

Today, I was snuggling Hudson, and he would touch his tracheostomy scar then touch my neck in the same spot. He did this over and over again. It made me so sad...I told him, "I know. It's not fair that you have that scar, and I don't. You have been through so much that is unfair."

The Holy Spirit began to convict me. How many times do I obsessively compare my scars to others? How much time and energy do I waste dwelling on the ugly scars and the unfairness? How often do I discount myself because I have too many scars?

Hudson's scars are proof that he has life. They are there, because they were the necessary means to keeping him alive.

Isn't that why mine are there? They are evidence that Jesus has done what is necessary to give me life (abundantly). They may not look like those of other people, but who cares? Christ has redeemed me and called me by name, and the scars I bear are evidence of Him at work in me. May I learn to recognize them as touches from His mighty hand.

Further Reading

Psalm 139:13-16, Titus 3:5-8, Isaiah 53:5

Journal Space

Post Op Thoughts

So tomorrow will be one week post-op for me, and I keep thinking about something.

Right after my surgery, the doctor asked how I was feeling. I told him that I couldn't believe how little pain I had. I wished I had not put the surgery off for so long.

His response..."Right. Well, we took out what was hurting you. Your pain now is small, because we had to cut things away. It hurts where they were attached. But the things that caused the 'bigger pain' aren't there anymore."

I just keep thinking about how this is me and sin sometimes. I wait and wait to do anything about it until sin has grown so big in my life it is causing tremendous pain. But I adjust and get used to the pain. I fear how badly it will hurt to let Jesus remove it. But then I begin having trouble walking the way I should and functioning as God intended...just like I was doing before my surgery.

When we ask God to forgive our sin and to remove it from us, He does it. And the big pain is gone. Sometimes there is "small pain"...learning to leave habits, relationships, thinking patterns etc. behind, but WE FEEL SO MUCH

BETTER...and we think "Why didn't I take care of this long ago?"

Lord, cut the things out of my life that are causing me to live less than the life You have for me. How ridiculous for me to live any other way.

Further Reading

Romans 6:23, Psalm 103, Colossians 1:13-14

Journal Space

A Sweet Reminder

Yesterday, after our morning church service, my family saw the sweetest reminder.

Our youth pastor had gathered up a sign/banner from the front of our church and was putting it away. He was walking in the back, carrying the bulk of it and its weight. In front, proudly marching and smiling (carrying just the tiniest part) was our youth pastor's little daughter.

It reminded me of what it looks like…us and Jesus. Jesus could carry the load without us – it would be easier and faster…more efficient and certainly less drama! But He invites us to be a part of what He is doing! We are carrying the tiniest little bit…He is the One getting the thing done…but the smile and sense of accomplishment and peace of being part of what He is doing that we experience are worth so much to Him.

Thank You, Lord, for using us in Your plans! You don't need us, but my what we get done when we are working with You!

Further Reading

Matthew 11:28-30, Psalm 55:22

Journal Space

Weariness

Jeremiah 31:25 "For I satisfy the weary ones and refresh everyone who languishes."

I am weary. I get the deepest meaning of that word. I even understand the many ways God satisfies me in the midst of my weariness.

But what does it mean to be refreshed when I am languishing?

To languish means to "suffer from being forced to remain in an unpleasant place or situation". Yep...been there...in my health, in my location, in my relationships, in my parenting. In.my.life. There may not be anything more miserable than being stuck and unable to free one's self. It is even worse if I have placed myself there.

So, what does it mean that the Lord will refresh me when I am languishing? We generally interpret that to mean that God gives us new strength or energy...He reinvigorates us. And I believe God absolutely does that.

But did you know that there is another definition of refresh? It also means to "stimulate or jog someone's memory by checking or going over previous information."

So, when I am weary and in a terrible place that I cannot get out of, God renews my strength...by reminding me...jogging my memory about what He has done previously...you see, we have a HIStory.

"Remember that year, Mindy, when you were so tired of trying to work through the foster care system to adopt? I woke you up at midnight every night to get on your face in your prayer closet to pray...and I brought you Amyra...and then Hudson."

"Remember that time that Amyra was blue and barely breathing? There was nothing you could do; you were helpless and afraid, but I healed her."

"Remember that time when you had bills due and no food to eat, and you didn't know what you were going to do? You walked outside, and there was money underneath your windshield wiper...just enough, and you made it."

"Remember that time you were at your wit's end with your daughter's behavior, and I prompted you to stop to pray? She looked at you and said, 'Can I ask Jesus in my heart right now? Will you help me, Mama?' "

Oh, Lord, thank You. There are just no words for Your refreshment in the midst of my languishing.

Further Reading

Lamentations 3:21-25, Psalm 77:11, Deuteronomy 6:6-12

Journal Space

The "Instead" Blessing

Have you ever prayed that God would bless you…and you make sure to let Him know how He should do it? I have been pondering this more and more over the last few weeks.

…How I asked Him to bless me with biological children…and "instead" He blessed me with two adopted children that are living, breathing miracles and draw me closer to Him every day.

…How I asked Him to let a relationship be "the one"…and "instead" He blessed me with a season of singleness when I learned to give my time, energy, money, efforts to Him first…some of the sweetest times in my life with Him.

…How I asked Him to bless us with a certain house in a certain neighborhood…and "instead" He blessed me with a different house in a neighborhood where my neighbors want to know more about Jesus and how to serve Him.

…How I asked Him for freedom from pain…and "instead" He blessed me with supernatural perseverance, endurance, and peace along with a fresh awareness of His presence.

…How I asked Him to heal my mama…and "instead" He healed her in heaven and blessed me with comfort through family and friends in brand new ways.

I think that I might stop asking Him to bless me "my" way. Lord, I want the "instead" blessings! Open my eyes to see You at work as You are continually blessing me. Don't let me miss a single one.

Further Reading

Proverbs 10:7, Ezekiel 34:26, Psalm 144:15

Journal Space

Lost Keys

Have you ever lost or misplaced your keys? Usually, it happens when you are in a hurry. You look everywhere, but you cannot seem to find them. It is so incredibly frustrating. Inevitably, someone says, "Where was the last place you remember having them?"

Well, sometimes, I feel like I have lost or misplaced God. I feel as though I cannot hear Him or see Him in my situation. It is so frustrating to need His wisdom and guidance but not be able to put my finger on it.

So, when that happens, I have begun asking myself the same question I ask when I lose my keys…"Where was the last place I remember 'having' Him?"

Then, I begin to recall how He was there guiding me when I changed jobs…the way He helped Jeff and I to decide to work to build our marriage together…when He guided us to adopt children that needed a lot of help…when He was my only comfort during my mom's illness and passing…and on and on the list goes.

I never lost Him, but because I was not stopping with a heart of gratitude and amazement to remember all He has done, I felt disconnected from Him. I never stopped praying or reading my Bible, but I had forgotten to recall what He had done for me PERSONALLY.

So, next time you think you cannot find God, remember…"Where was the last place you had Him?"

Further Reading

Deuteronomy 4:29, 2 Chronicles 26:5, Psalm 63:1, Colossians 3:1

Journal Space

Loss

A dear friend has been keeping vigil with her mom as she prepares to meet Jesus. She has been tenderly holding her mom's hand.

Her journey has reminded me of my mom and her hands.

…all the times when I was young that my mom held my hand walking across a street or parking lot to keep me safe

…the time I broke up with a boyfriend and my mom came to pick me up, comforting me by holding my hand in the back seat for the 45-minute ride home

…the time my mom reached out to hold my hand as she prayed for a blessing over my marriage on my wedding day.

…the time I held my mom's hand and told her it was okay to go meet Jesus, comforting us both with a few last moments of holding each other's hand

It is so hard to let go. But I read Mark 9:27 this morning. "But Jesus took him by the hand and raised him; and he got up."

When we think we have too much to bear, when we have lost too much, when we are so alone and miss the hands of those we love dearly, Jesus holds our hand. And then, we can get up.

Thank You, Jesus.

Further Reading

Psalm 18:35, Psalm 20:6, Matthew 8:3, Matthew 9:25

Journal Space

Who Is Driving?

Amyra and I have very different pigments (she being African American and I being Caucasian), but sometimes we look so alike...

Today, we were headed to yet another appointment, and Amyra piped up from the back seat...

"Mom, you are a really good driver! I don't always know where we are going, but I trust you. I love riding around with you!"

I thought, "What a sweet girl I have." Then I looked in the rear-view mirror, and she had a circular piece of plastic held up like a steering wheel. She was making every turn!

Lord, that's me. I tell You how good You are...that I trust You to drive this thing called "my life". But I am in the back seat holding my "steering wheel" trying to control every turn we make...when I really should be enjoying riding with You, trusting You (even when I don't know where we are going).

You are in control, Lord. I really do trust You. Please help me "ride" in peace, living out that trust.

Further Reading

Hebrews 2:13, Daniel 6, Isaiah 12:2

Journal Space

Getting More Involved

Just a thought...

You keep saying you want to do more at church. You want to be more involved, have more responsibility.

There's the mom down the aisle from you who works long hours. She is a single mom. How about surprising her with dinner for her family?

There's the mom in your Sunday school class who is overwhelmed with her kids and other relatives that she is caring for. How about volunteering to babysit once in a while?

And there's a dad dropping off his baby in the nursery who just got divorced. The weekends when he doesn't have the baby are hard. Why not invite him to your house for dinner on one of those weekends?

And then there's the single woman at the welcome desk who is all alone in town. Why not call her up to meet for a cup of coffee?

Oh, I forgot. You are too busy trying to get more involved at church.

Further Reading

John 15:12, Romans 12:10, Galatians 5:13

Journal Space

Esther Part One

Our family is studying the book of Esther together, and I noticed something that I have missed in previous studies of this book.

The story begins in the third year of the king's reign. Esther comes to the palace in the seventh year of his reign, and Haman finally starts his plan of revenge in the twelfth year of the king's reign. This is not a fast-moving story!

I wonder if Esther had started to feel (after 5 years in the palace) that God had forgotten her. Did she wonder why she still could not see His plan for having her there? Did she think that she had heard God incorrectly? Did she wonder if He had a purpose for her after all? Was she tired of seeking Him, asking Him to show her why she was there and what she was supposed to be doing?

Can you relate? I can! Sometimes it seems like I have been "here" waiting for Him to show me "why" for such a long, long time. I wonder why I have been placed in a set of circumstances and why I cannot always clearly see Him at work.

But, Esther has encouraged me anew. God has put me "here" for "such a time as this", and just because it is not going as quickly as I had imagined does not mean that He has forgotten His plan. He will accomplish His will, and I am so thankful to be a part of it. I will pray that He continues to remind me that I am on His schedule. I will wait expectantly to see His plan unfold.

Further Reading

Esther 1-5

Journal Space

Esther Part Two

We are still studying Esther as a family, and we are still amazed by what God is teaching us.

Esther spoke up for her people, and the king gave her and Mordecai the authority to declare that the Jewish people could defend themselves against their attackers.

God did not take away the problem. People still attacked them.

When I ask God for deliverance and rescue, I am really asking for my problem to be taken away. Often, He says no to that. He just gives me the strength to fight, and He stands with me in the situation. I am never the same afterward.

So, let's praise Him for all the times that He did not change our circumstances, but instead changed us. Hallelujah!

Further Reading

Esther 6-10

Journal Space

Judgment

I have been upset today. Amyra confided that a "friend" has been routinely critical and unkind to her. I was so hurt and angry on her behalf. She is such a sweet, loving girl. I was incensed that someone who was supposed to love her could treat her this way.

And then, the Holy Spirit began to convict my heart. "Mindy, do you ever judge those around you? Are you unkind in your thoughts to your fellow believers...the ones you are supposed to love? Maybe you don't say it as plainly to them as Amyra's 'friend', but you subtly let them know that they aren't measuring up to your standards. Don't you know that I love them even more than you love Amyra? Don't you know that it breaks my heart to seem them hurting at your treatment of them? And it hurts to see you be uncaring of others...even unintentionally."

Forgive me, Lord. Thank You for reminding me that You love us all, imperfect though we all may be. Thank You for reminding me that I should see Jesus when I look at others...that's what You see when You look at me. Help me to teach my children to see people this way. Amyra always says, "Love means hugging someone even if they don't deserve it."

P.S. Someone should really warn you ahead of time that having kids is extremely convicting!

Further Reading

Matthew 7:2, Luke 6:37, I Samuel 16:7

Journal Space

Gifts

Someone very dear to me once shared a story. It has come to my mind several times lately, so I thought I would share.

Things had been difficult in this person's family, and at Christmas time that year money was tight. They received a single present, a game, to share with two other siblings. After opening the gift, they looked at their mother and said, "Is that all?" My loved one weeps every time…describing the pain on their mom's face. She had done her best, and it was not enough for them.

How often do you think Christ has that look on His face…when He has given me His all, His best and I say, "Is that all?"? All too often, I look down upon the gifts He has given me (life, salvation, love, joy, peace, family, mercy, grace, etc.). He who has given me everything (all of which is more than I can or could ever deserve) must be so pained by my reaction. And Christ has not given out of meager resources! He has given out of the abundance that is God's!

Oh, Lord! Let me never again look at a gift from You and ask if that is all. May I look at every gift with gratitude and joy, because it came from You. Even when I do not understand the gift, let me trust the Giver.

Further Reading

John 3:16, Luke 11:13, I Corinthians 15:57, Isaiah 25:1

Journal Space

My Ancestry

I love history. I love reading about the past and how it has shaped the present. I love the show "Finding Your Roots"...people finding out about ancestors and family history they never knew.

I know some of my ancestry (thanks to my Uncle Al Cariker and my Nana Ketchum). I have even taken an ethnicity DNA test to learn more details.

I also keep track of as much family history for my two children as I can. Since they are adopted, there are a lot of unknowns. I try to fill the gaps as I am able, so they will know as much as possible.

Inevitably, people on the ancestry shows say something like "I never knew who I was" or "I am glad to know where I come from".

Their responses always make me think. There is no mystery. I know who I am. I am a sinner. And no matter where I or my family originated, my identity (and salvation!) are found in the One who has redeemed me and called me by His name. I am a child of the King. Low born or high born, rich or poor, white or black, free or slave, He gave His life to make me His.

No wondering about it. I know Whose I am. Hallelujah!

Further Reading

John 1:12, Romans 8:16-21, Ephesians 5:1, I John 3:1a, I John 5:1

Journal Space

Thankful Heart

I had a conversation with my dad this morning, and after I hung up I realized I had forgotten to tell him thank you for something he had helped me do.

It made me think. Is there Someone else I am talking with and forgetting to thank?

Do you ever find your prayers going like this…" Lord, I need…Help me with…I want…"?

Where is my thankful heart? The Almighty God hears my prayers. Jesus paid the price for my sins with His life. There has never been a time when my true needs have not been met by His gracious hand.

HOW COULD I FORGET TO THANK HIM?

Forgive me, Lord. You above all others deserve my gratitude and devotion and praise. Help my forgetful heart to live in continual awe of all the ways You show Your love for me, and help me to tell You thank You…not because You need to hear it, but because I need to say it.

Further Reading

I Chronicles 16:34, 2 Samuel 22:50, Psalm 117, Psalm 150

Journal Space

My Right to Complain

Life is complicated at times, and it often seems unfair. Things go wrong when we have done all the right things.

I have thought many times "I want to complain. I DESERVE to complain!" But 2 Samuel 19:28b says, "What right do I have yet that I should complain anymore to the King?"

The King Who has saved me…Who loves me as His own…Who gives me all good things.

When we are tempted to complain (because God is not responding quickly enough or favorably enough to suit us), may we stop and imagine what He, in His infinite grace and mercy, has already done for us today (or saved us from) that we may never know about till heaven.

And then, may we fall on our faces in gratitude and humility before our King.

Further Reading

Colossians 3:12, James 1:21, Isaiah 4:6, 2 Thessalonians 3:3

Journal Space

Adoption

When we were going through the process of adopting Amyra, we were very new to foster care and the adoption process.

Our social worker told us that one of the last things that we would do before the adoption would be final was "disclosure".

She brought in 1,100 pages of documentation. It listed every physical, mental, medical, behavioral, family, etc. problem that was known about our sweet Amyra. We had to read every word and then sign papers saying we still wanted to adopt her.

I thought "Of course we still want her! There is nothing you could say about this baby that would make me want to give her back!"

And the Holy Spirit whispered to me "That's how I feel about you, Mindy...about all of you. You can bring me all the mess and problems in your life and lay it all out before me, but there is nothing you could do or say that would make me turn away from wanting to adopt you into my family."

What a mess we often are, but there is nothing His love cannot cover...nothing that can separate us from Him.

Further Reading

Romans 8:15 and 31-39, John 3:16-17, Galatians 2:20 and 4:5, Ephesians 1:5

Journal Space

Not "Lord, help me bear up"

Instead "Lord, bear it"

I have been overwhelmed by some recent tasks laid before me. I have not felt up to the challenge. I have prayed (like I always have) "Lord, give me the strength to bear up under this pressure. I want to accomplish these tasks. I am at 75%, Lord. Please give me that other 25%!"

Today, the Lord gently reminded me that I keep asking Him to give, give, give. And He often does. But, this time, why don't I try asking Him to take? "Lord, take this burden. Don't help me to bear it with more grace and energy. TAKE IT!"

The situation hasn't changed. I still have obligations. But the Lord took my burden. Now, it is His, and I am just praying He will show me where and how He wants to use me…to accomplish this task for HIS glory, in HIS way, in HIS time.

(And, to be fair, the 75% I thought I had was really from Him anyway.)

"Cast all your cares on Him. He will make you His personal concern." I Peter 5:7 CEV

Further Reading

Psalm 71, Isaiah 30:15, Exodus 33:14

Journal Space

Waiting for a Call

I have been waiting for a week for a phone call from a specialist's office to set up an appointment. I knew that I would not have answers yet, but it would be a relief to get an appointment on the books – to get the ball rolling.

After not hearing anything for a week, I made a series of phone calls. Eventually, I found out that the specialist's office had been told I would call them (I had been told they would contact me), and they were waiting on ME!

This is how it has been with me and the Lord many times. I am waiting on the Lord to show up and do something when He has been waiting on me to "call" Him to ask.

And just like the relief of making an appointment to get things started, turning to the Lord in prayer does not immediately solve my problems. But it brings immediate relief when I make an appointment to turn over my concerns to God in prayer.

The best thing about the Lord is that He doesn't wait on me to call Him to start working on my issues. He has been working all along. My prayers just open my eyes and ears to see and hear what He is doing. And He is doing much.

Further Reading

Jeremiah 33:3, Psalm 145:18, Romans 10:13

Journal Space

Doctor's Office

Sitting in the doctor's office today reminded me of church.

Some women were getting ultrasounds of their babies. Some women were getting check-ups. Some women were there to plan their surgeries.

All in the same place but for very different reasons.

Church is the same way. Some are there to praise. Some are there because they are hurting. Some are there because they don't know where else to go.

All in the same place for very different reasons.

But just like my doctor was prepared to deal with all the patients he saw, regardless of the issue, God can meet every single need we could ever have. There is nothing for which He doesn't have the answer.

I just wish we were better at sharing the highs and lows of those in "the waiting room" with us. It never hurts to share one another's burdens and to remind each other that we have come to the right place for His help.

Further Reading

Philippians 4:19, I Corinthians 2:9, Ephesians 2:10

Journal Space

The Right Way

On our way to the salon this morning, Amyra said, "Mom, this is NOT the way to the salon! I have been there, and I KNOW the way! Are we lost?"

I replied, "Honey, it isn't time for us to be there yet, so I am taking you the long way. Have I ever gotten you lost before? We will get there. I promise."

Then the Holy Spirit said, "That's you, Mindy. You think you know the way your path should be going. You don't understand that it's not time for you to get 'there' yet. Have I ever gotten you lost before? You will get where you are supposed to be when you are supposed to be there. I promise."

Lord, I confess I like to know ahead of time what Your plan is. Help me to rest in Your promise of accomplishing Your good will in my life. I KNOW You always do what You say You will do!

Further Reading

Proverbs 16:9, Proverbs 19:21, Psalm 33:11

Journal Space

Weakness

Today, I am once again reminded that God's provision often does not look like I wish it to look, but He always provides.

I would have preferred to have an able body today, capable of all the tasks needing my attention. Instead, God provided loved ones to accomplish the tasks that could not be rescheduled.

What a reminder to look to Him for all my needs (not myself).

Reminds me of the Scripture I read at my mom's service a few years ago…"And He said to me, 'My grace is sufficient for you, for My strength is made perfect in weakness.' Therefore most gladly I will rather boast in my infirmities, that the power of Christ may rest upon me."

I am complete when I am weak, because then His grace and strength have room to take over.

Thank You, Lord, for helping me get out of my own way today. I need You every day, not just when things are difficult. Help me to write that on the tablet of my heart and to remember.

Further Reading

Psalm 37:25-26, Matthew 6:25-34

Journal Space

Miracles

Sometimes, I am tempted to forget that God still does miracles. My circumstances seem overwhelming at times.

But then I think of Amyra and Hudson.

Amyra was born at 25 weeks, weighing 1 pound 13 ounces. We were told that she had little chance of walking, eating, or breathing on her own. She had been deprived of oxygen at least three times and had a serious heart defect. She had 6 surgeries before age two.

Hudson was born at 34 weeks, weighing 2 pounds 5 ounces. His biological mother was an alcoholic, and this resulted in Hudson's fetal alcohol syndrome and the death of his twin sister. We were told not to expect much from him. He had at least 13 surgeries by age two and a half.

But then, God.

As I write this, Amyra is a completely normal and healthy 6-year-old, and Hudson has recently tested as age appropriate in all areas. They still have their challenges (as we all do), but God uses them often to show off!

Amyra's doctor told her "I have seen many premature little ones, Amyra. Being born so early, you shouldn't be able to do everything you can do. You are amazing!"

Amyra's reply… "GOD is amazing!"

Hudson's doctor was surprised at his progress during his last check-up. She asked him, "What have you been doing, Hudson?"

And the boy who rarely speaks, smiled and said "God."

God still does miracles. Shame on us for being surprised that He is the God He says He is.

I don't know what miracle you need today. But He knows. And He is able!

Further Reading

Ephesians 3:20-21, Daniel 3, Hebrews 7:2, Hebrews 11:19

The Woman at the Well

We were studying the woman at the well story today in Bible class (homeschool). I looked over at the coloring page Amyra was doing, and I could tell she was upset.

"I drew sin on her with a pencil. Now, I cannot get it all the way off – even though I erased it. I can still see it. I tried coloring over the 'sin', but no matter what I do, I can't get rid of it. I guess I just need to face it – I am NOT Jesus!"

I laughed at first. Then I began to think about all the times I tried to cover/hide my sin. Or gloss over the sin of myself or others…all the times I tried to make change happen in my heart or the heart of another.

Let's just face it. We are not Jesus. We need Him to blot out our sins and make us white as snow again. No one else, no other method will do…only the One who died to pay for and to forgive our sins and to give us abundant life can do it.

Why am I wasting my time instead of giving it to Him?

(P.S. I gave her another coloring page. She said it was just like Jesus wiping us clean, so we could start fresh. Lord, let me get it the way she does.)

Further Reading

John 4, Isaiah 1:18

Journal Space

My Name

Did you ever notice that Eve was given her name (by Adam) AFTER she had eaten the fruit?

Goodness, that speaks to me! After I have messed up or failed or done the same wrong thing yet again, I feel like I have a "name". Failure, loser, weak, never-changing, discouragement, hindrance...and the list could go on and on.

How about you? Is there a "name" you have been given? Or given yourself? Are you identifying yourself by what you have or have not done?

Well, the Bible is pretty clear about the Name God sees when He looks at us believers.

"...for I have redeemed you; I have called you by name; you are Mine!" Isaiah 43:1b

So, let's see what He calls us...

Redeemed (Isaiah 43 and many more)

Not Condemned (Romans 8:1)

Adopted (Galatians 4:5)

Blessed and Forgiven (Romans 4:7)

And on and on it goes...

I am a child of the King. That is my name! And no other name I have been given holds up to that one!

Further Reading

Genesis 3 (verse 20), Isaiah 43, Romans 4 and 8,

Galatians 4

Journal Space

Holding Hands Journal Space

Today, while walking with Amyra, I had to stop often to tell her not to hold my hand so tightly or pull on my arm so hard. We had been several places, and every time we got out of the car or elevator, she would grip me with all of her might.

Finally, exasperated, I said, "Baby! You don't have to hold on to me! I am holding on to YOU!"

And then the Holy Spirit whispered, "Hey, Mindy. That's the deal. It's not about how hard you hang onto Me. It's about My hanging onto you. And I have promised to never leave you or forsake you."

Resting better tonight.

Further Reading

Deuteronomy 31:6-8, Hebrews 13:5b, Nehemiah 9:31

A New Thing

I wish that I could wake up every morning with a new a specific word from God. Something like "Mindy, today, you will go to the grocery store. Then, you will call your friend and encourage her. You will follow that with writing a card to another friend. Before you go to bed, I want you to get on your face to pray. The doorbell will ring with a surprise from Me!"

In other words, I wish He would spell it all out for me! I want Him to make a list of my priorities...probably so I don't have to try to listen to figure out what He is asking of me.

But "Whatever you have learned or heard from Me, or seen in Me put it into practice; and the God of peace will be with you."
Philippians 4:9

I don't need new instructions or a fresh revelation or a glimpse of the future to have His peace.

I just need to be obedient in the old things...the things He has already told me to do. Things like praying, reading God's Word and hiding it in my heart, loving my neighbors, giving generously, etc.

Further Reading

Philippians 4:9, 2 Timothy 3:14, Revelation 2:25

Journal Space

Stooping Down

This week, I had yet another post-op check-up. I am feeling more myself...which means I am getting frustrated with some of the restrictions the doctor has recommended.

Like bending over.

There has been a piece of paper in the middle of the living room floor for 7 days 11 hours and 32 minutes.

And I cannot bend over to pick it up.

I will admit that I have dwelled on that paper A LOT.

I was nearly to the point of breaking the rules and bending over to pick it up. Then I thought "Wait...you are going to jeopardize your whole recovery and healing by stooping down for a piece of paper? How ridiculous!"

Then I thought about how I sometimes do that very thing in my spiritual life. I ask God to do "surgery" to weed out the sin and unhealthy things in my life, but I get fixated on the one distraction or temptation until I am ready to jeopardize

what He has done and the progress I have made to stoop down to pick up a habit or a relationship or a whatever.

Lord, I don't want to go back to how I lived before. Let me keep my eyes on You and away from the insignificant things. Remind me not to stoop down for the things that do not matter.

Further Reading

Psalm 51, Titus 2:14, James 4:8

Journal Space

Eye Surgery

My husband Jeff was going to have eye surgery. He has a progressive eye disease that has been worsening, and the doctors hoped that the procedure would halt the progression of the disease and prevent further surgical needs (like a cornea transplant).

I was afraid. Jeff's eyes are vital to what he does, and he is our bread winner. I found myself praying for peace but continually bringing this up to the Lord…"God, nothing can go wrong. We need his income! We can't make it without it. What would we do if he permanently lost his sight? We have seen this devastate other!"

And the Holy Spirit gently reminded me, "Yes, Mindy. Jeff is your bread winner. But I am your Provider."

Truth. Anything we have or have ever had has been provided by HIM. Neither Jeff nor I have done anything to earn our abilities. They are gifts from our Provider. The opportunities and positions we have had are from HIM. The strength and health we enjoy are provision from His hand.

I was still nervous but no longer afraid. I knew God would provide no matter what. He always has.

Further Reading

Philippians 4:6-7, Psalm 56:3, Psalm 34:4

Journal Space

Time Together

Amyra was driving me crazy one day. Everywhere I went, everything I did, there she was. In exasperation, I looked at her and asked, "Why do you seem to be everywhere I am today?"

She replied, "How am I going to learn how to be like you if we don't spend a lot of time together?"

Exactly. If I want to be like Jesus, how am I ever going to do it if I don't spend time with Him...in His Word...in prayer? Do I really want to be more like Him? Are the places I am investing my time and resources a reflection of my desire for Him or something else?

Lord, let me never forget that time together is how I will learn to be like You...and how my children will learn to be like You, too.

"Make me know Your ways, O LORD; Teach me Your paths. Lead me in Your truth and teach me, for You are the God of my salvation; for You I wait all the day."
Psalm 25:4 and 5

Further Reading

Psalm 25, Psalm 119

Journal Space

Hip Helpers

When our son Hudson first came to live with us, he was not able to do much physically. He couldn't sit up, crawl, hold a toy etc. We consulted many doctors and therapists to help us devise strategies and exercises that would help him make steady progress with his motor skills.

One of the most recommended helps was "hip helpers". They are very constricting shorts that force the child's legs to stay together in the position needed to sit on one's own and to crawl. They help the child's muscle tone; however, they are tight and made out of material that does not "breathe".

Needless to say, every time we put them on Hudson, he would cry and squirm and whine. He didn't understand that the constriction he was experiencing was to teach him how to develop the skills that would enable him to achieve walking...freedom. The temporary discomfort was necessary for his future good.

Sound familiar? It does to me! I often whine and complain about the discomforts of life and its various trials, when God is trying to tell me, "This is developing skills in you for your future good and freedom!" Spiritual muscle tone!

Lord, help me to see every situation and circumstance that comes my way as a divine opportunity to build my spiritual muscles. Remind me that You are using ALL of these things for my good.

"And we know that God causes all things to work together for good to those who love God, to those who are called according to His purpose." Romans 8:28

Further Reading

Philippians 1:6, Psalm 143:10, Psalm 116:12, Romans 6:22, Romans 8:28

The Stars

Journal Space

This has been a rough week, but tonight, when we got home from church, Amyra said, "Mom, look at all those stars! Why can we see them so clearly here but not other places?"

I answered, "We are away from town now and all those lights. The darker it is, the brighter the stars seem to shine and the better we can see them."

Oh.

Thank You, Jesus, for shining so brightly in our darkness. Thank You for letting us see You more clearly the darker things seem to be.

And thank You for reminding me of that tonight.

Further Reading

John 8:12, John 12:46, Luke 2:32, Psalm 18:28

My Hope

Amyra and I were talking tonight, and she was listing all of the items she needed to complete a particular collection. I asked her, "What happens when you get them all?" She paused and said, "Then I will start collecting something else!"

"Babe," I said "There will always be the next thing. If you aren't careful you will never be satisfied. There will always be the next thing to hope for."

But what am I hoping for? What are you hoping for? A better house or car? A new job? To lose a few pounds? To have a little more money in the bank? An end of problems? None of those things are wrong, but they will never satisfy.

My hope in Christ is the only hope that fills my soul. He is the only thing that never disappoints. And our hope in Him is a sure thing…"This hope we have as an anchor of the soul, a hope both sure and steadfast…" (Hebrews 6:19)

Like the song says…

"My hope is built on nothing less than Jesus' blood and righteousness;

…On Christ the solid Rock I stand; all other ground is sinking sand."

Further Reading

Psalm 31:24, Psalm 42:5, Ephesians 1:18-23

Journal Space

Faith

Amyra once told me that if I prayed hard enough, God would make my skin brown like hers. I used to think that was the very definition of "faith like a child"...believing He can do the impossible or the improbable.

But I think it is more than that...it is believing He can do wonders in the mundane things, too.

I can easily let things in life cause me stress. Sometimes, caring for those I love weighs me down with the vastness of all that the responsibility entails. Sometimes, I am just bogged down with thoughts of how far I still have to go. I would dearly love to return to being a child some days!

Maybe that is one of the reasons Jesus says we must have the faith of a child. We must let go of all the worries and return to that child-like state...where our Father takes care of us, and we have nothing to do but smile at His love and goodness (and say thank You).

Lord, when the burdens of life seem too much, thank You for reminding me that You are my Father, and I am simply Your child. All that concerns me is carried in the palm of Your hand.

Further Reading

John 14:27, Luke 17:5, Luke 7:50, Romans 1:16-17

Journal Space

My Dad

I am so thankful for my dad.

I remember learning how to sacrifice by watching him give things to people that cost him much. He gave away things such as our Sunday lunch to a family that didn't have anything to eat, and he also gave things like money and cars – knowing it didn't seem like he could afford it, but that God always provides (and He did).

He also taught me the value of hard work. When I was a teenager, I had some gaps in my front teeth that induced a lot of insecurity in me. Braces were not going to help, but bonding the teeth would make them look good. There was no money for that. So, my dad worked out a deal with the dentist to do several weeks of electrical work (after his regular job) at night in the dental facility to pay for the bonding of my teeth.

I have been thinking how much my dad has always proved that he loves me…how he shows that he loves others. And I have been thinking that as great as my dad is, his love is just a drop in the bucket when compared with how much God loves me and how much He has done to prove His love for me.

I am completely overwhelmed by Him and His goodness. And I am so thankful for the earthly example of my dad…what it looks like to serve others in the name of Jesus.

Further Reading

Jeremiah 31:3, Psalm 103:17-18, Psalm 118, Psalm 136

Journal Space

Vacation

Seeing so many vacation photos lately has got me thinking. Sometimes, I try so hard to make good memories with friends and family. I want to always remember how much we love each other and all the things we have done and places we have been.

But, then I remember my mom…and her dementia. And I wonder what good making all those memories meant for her. In the end, what did she really know?

She knew Jesus. Only Jesus. And when her memories of our family Christmases and vacations and birthdays grew dim, Jesus continued to shine brightly. Once, when my parents stopped at a stop sign, Mom began to sing "Stop and tell the story of what the Lord has done for you."

So, I will take my family trips. I will make all the memories that I can with my loved ones. But I will make sure Jesus is there, in the forefront. Because, in the end, it is Jesus. Only Jesus.

Further Reading

I John 3:22-24

Journal Space

Worthy

Awhile back, I found out that one of our health care professionals (upon finding out we would be adopting another medically fragile child) commented, "Why would you want a used car when you could have a new car?"

I was furious and completely indignant! How dare he?! These children are special gifts! How dare he belittle them?!

Then the Holy Spirit said, "Do you ever do that, Mindy? Do you ever think that some people are too much trouble, too messy, not worth it? Do you treat them like they are gifts? Always? Does Jesus treat you like that?

I am so convicted and so thankful. God's love, guidance, sacrifice, grace, and mercy leave no doubt about the special gift and priceless worth He sees when He looks at me.

Lord, let me see others the way You do!

Further Reading

Ephesians 2:4-9, Matthew 10:31, Isaiah 43:4, Luke 12:6-7

Journal Space

Generosity

When we have a lot, it is easy to give. But when we have a mortgage, medical bills, car repair bills, and our job cuts down our hours, giving seems a little out of reach.

There is more to being generous than giving money and things though. We can be generous with our time, our praise, our grace and mercy. We can generously forgive in kindness. We can be generously thoughtful and considerate. Generously put the other person first.

We must be generous with all that God has given us. He has given all of these things to us to give away. And since He GAVE it to us, it doesn't cost us a thing to give it to others.

He always gives more to us...our cups overflow.

And as the wise sage Amyra says, "Our love (generosity) needs legs!"

Further Reading

Romans 6:6-9, 2 Corinthians 8:2-3, Luke 6:38

Journal Space

The Difficult Things

Amyra asked me why Grandma (my mom) died. I said, "She was sick for a very long time, and Jesus decided it was time for her to get to go to heaven where she would never be sick again."

Her reply…"That's so nice. I just love Jesus!"

Not my initial reaction, I will admit. I wanted Him to restore her health. I wanted more years with her.

I rarely stopped to see the kindness in Jesus in allowing her to go home.

Is there something today that is not what you wanted of Him? Does it seem so very hard to bear or understand?

Look for the kindness of Him in that thing. It is there, because He loves You so much. Look through your tears to His face.

He is so nice. I just love Jesus.

Further Reading

I Chronicles 16:34, Psalm 13:5, Psalm 26:3, Psalm 36:5, Psalm 63:3

Journal Space

Expectations

Hudson has been sequestered and not allowed out for a few weeks, but his physical therapist and speech pathologist have been allowed in to work with him.

Yesterday, about halfway through physical therapy time, he looked at me...looked at the therapist...and signed "All done!" quite emphatically.

We both laughed, and then we teared up. Not many people gave Hudson much hope of doing anything (not moving, eating, speaking, thinking, etc.), but here he was walking, exercising, and cognitively aware of how to tell us that he had worked hard enough!

How like God to do so much more than we expected (and He isn't done yet)!

What is it in your life you think cannot be changed or fixed or redeemed or forgiven? God is in the business of doing so much more than we can think of or imagine (Ephesians 3:20).

Let's start EXPECTING miracles instead of being surprised by them. We are not able, but we serve a mighty God who is!

Further Reading

Psalm 24:8, Deuteronomy 3:24, Psalm 89:8, Joshua 4:24

Journal Space

Preparation

When Joseph was 17, he lived at home. God gave him a dream, but he had to go through family issues, slavery, imprisonment, and some more family issues before the dream came to pass (when Joseph was 40 or so years old).

God had to make Joseph WHO He wanted him to be, before Joseph could arrive WHERE he needed to be.

God is using all the turmoil in our lives to prepare us for greater things. And often we can look back in amazement at how God has prepared us for things we never could have seen coming.

When I was 6, my family moved to Spencer, OK. That community was predominantly African-American, and I learned all kinds of things about skin care and hair care from a culture different from my own.

When I was 14, I felt God calling me to adopt. I read every story and article about adoption I could find.

When I was in junior high and high school, I became fascinated with medical journals. I read them at the library and anywhere else I could find them. My mom had some health struggles at the time, so I assumed I was curious because of her.

Now, I am the adoptive mother of two medically fragile children…one of whom is African-American. I am able to comprehend their medical conditions easily, and much of Amyra's skin and hair care came easily as well. Because God knew what was coming even when I had no idea.

God plans a path for us. He uses EVERYTHING for our good. Don't take for granted the place or season or passion that currently occupies your time. If you will surrender to Him, He will use even the most "random" things for His plan. Nothing is wasted in His economy.

Further Reading

Joseph's story (Genesis 37-45)

Journal Space

My Portion

Jeremiah was a prophet who was used to speaking about the future. When he wrote Lamentations, he suddenly began speaking about the present time. Josiah (holy king) had died. Judah and Jerusalem were lost. God's people were turning away again. As far as his eyes could see, there was chaos and turmoil. Jeremiah could not see past the current circumstance to the future. Captivity for God's people.

Sound like us and our world? Our nation celebrates sin, legalizes murder, suppresses/persecutes the Word and those who would share it. Our world is lost and starving...brutally mistreated...new atrocities in the news every day. Our churches are often focused on projects and programs instead of people. And we are frequently so inwardly focused on making sure we have "enough" that we ignore our neighbors (other than to make sure we are appearing more successful than they...keeping up with the Joneses). We are more concerned with appearing well than being well.

But in the midst of all this, we read what Jeremiah says in Lamentations 3:24 "The LORD is my portion, saith my soul; therefore will I hope in Him."

Portion – what does that mean? If someone give you a portion of cake, it is a slice that you eat and then it is gone. If someone leaves you a portion of their estate as an inheritance, you receive part of their money...gone once it is spent. You give an allowance or portion to your children...and we all know how long that lasts!

And of course, we are all familiar with "portion-control" dieting...there is never enough when one is on that plan!

But when God says HE is our portion, that means He Himself and His eternal, boundless resources are ours! 2 Corinthians 9:8 says "God is able to make ALL grace abound to you, so that having ALL sufficiency in ALL things at ALL times, you may abound in every (ALL) good work."

We will never use up all that God is. We will never run out of His goodness, His mercy, His grace, His truth, His love, His forgiveness, His joy, His peace, His gentleness, His sovereignty, His faithfulness, His hope, His ANYTHING.

He is our ALL IN ALL. He is our Portion. Whatever it is you need, He has it...and He will never run out.

We run out of patience with our children (and spouses). We run out of time...to accomplish tasks or to spend with our loved ones. We run out of money. We run out of hope...that our nation will change, that our world will be saved, that our small contributions will make a difference, that we will survive our current situations.

But with Jesus as our portion...we have HOPE. We have it ALL.

Further Reading

Lamentations 3

Journal Space

Stewardship

When my husband and I were praying about having children, I would wake up every night at midnight. I felt an overwhelming urge to get on my face in our bedroom closet to pray.

I would get on the floor and start to ask God about giving us children. Each and every time, the Holy Spirit whispered to me "What about stewardship?"

I was confused. We tithed faithfully, and we were generous with our time and talents. Why was God speaking to me about stewardship?

Finally, one night, I felt Him speak to my spirit, "You are not a good steward of your body. You are making poor choices with something I have given you to care for. Why should I give you more?"

I felt so absolutely convicted. The next day, I began to make healthier eating choices and to exercise. And one year later, we brought Amyra home.

Did God care about how much I weighed? Maybe. But He did care about my loving and caring for every single thing He had given me, and I believe He rewarded my obedience...with better health and some sweet children on loan from Him.

Whatever it is...health of body, finances, emotions, resources of any kind are only given to us to bring Him glory. So, how can we feel good doing less than that?

Further Reading

Psalm 24:1, I Chronicles 29:12, Colossians 3:23-24

Journal Space

Be Still

I homeschool my children, and I really love it.

But Amyra is not a naturally calm child. One day, she was running around during a break in class time. She was yelling to entertain her brother and making funny faces.

When it was time for us to resume our lessons, I tried to get her attention. She was oblivious. I tried again…and again…until I finally raised my voice to say, "Amyra, it is time to learn! BE STILL!"

She completely ignored me! Then, to my horror, I saw a very large spider right next to her bare foot.

"Amyra, be still! There is a huge spider right next to you."

Well, that got her attention! And it got mine as well.

How many times is the Lord asking me to be still so He can teach me something? Or so I can avoid a dangerous situation? Why do I wait so long to listen?

Lord, help me to hear You the first time You speak to me. Let me learn what You want me to learn and let me avoid the dangerous things You see on my path. Let me be still.

Further Reading

Psalm 46:10, Psalm 37:7, Exodus 14:14

Journal Space

God's Power

Luke 8:40-48 talks about a woman who had suffered for 12 years with a physical issue. She had tried everything to find relief and healing. She had been made unclean by this health issue, unable to go to the temple or worship with friends and family.

Ever feel this way? You have stuff that is keeping you apart? You have tried everything to fix it, but nothing has worked.

Well, the woman in this passage touched Jesus as He walked by. That word "touched" literally means "to fasten one's self to something; a death grip". She didn't just go to church and say "Great sermon and music!" and then go home and forget about it. She was hanging on to Him for dear life! And she was healed!

Do you want healing? Relief? Then hang on to Him! He is the only way and our only hope. That woman knew it...and if we are honest, we know it, too.

Time to start living like we believe it.

Further Reading

Luke 8 (lots of miracles)

Journal Space

Made in the USA
Coppell, TX
20 April 2022